AND THE WEATHER REMAINS THE SAME

poems by

Natalie Kimbell

Finishing Line Press
Georgetown, Kentucky

AND THE WEATHER REMAINS THE SAME

ACKNOWLEDGMENTS

"The Fish;" "Why I Still Struggle with a Cloudless Sky;" "And the Weather
Remains the Same;" "Our Fab Four;" "Trying to Explain How to Survive…"
in *Mildred Haun Review*
"At the Sequatchie Valley Overlook…" in *Beautiful in the Eye of the Beholder*
Anthology
"Never Say Never;" "Driving Up Lewis Chapel Mountain…" in *Tennessee
Voices*
"Mariposa de la Muerte" in *Abyss and Apex*
"Ghosts;" in *Pine Mountain Sand and Gravel*
"What We Accept" in *Artemis*
"Bar Room Meditation (Sean's Tavern)" in *Rye Whiskey Review*
"When the Universe Offers a Sign" in *Re/View*
"Spellbound" in *Shift*

Publisher: Leah Huete de Maines
Editor: Christen Kincaid
Cover Art and Design: Stephanie Tate
Author Photo: Beverly Key
Cover Design: Elizabeth Maines McCleavy

Order online: www.finishinglinepress.com
also available on amazon.com

Author inquiries and mail orders:
Finishing Line Press
PO Box 1626
Georgetown, Kentucky 40324
USA

Contents

"Storms don't come to teach us painful lessons, rather they were meant to wash us clean." —Shannon L. Alder

*To my teacher, my mentor, and my friend, the late
Linda Cline Ewton, who will remain to all those whose life
she touched, an example of what all teachers should strive to be.*

Hope in Dead Leaves

In remembrance of Poet and Teacher, Bill Brown

New tree buds will assuage parched
leaves from their marcescent vigil.
But today, winter dominates, cloaked
in the brisk chill of December.

In defiance to this season's reign
at Fall Creek Falls State Park, I perch
on a picnic table scarred with hearted initials,
a blank-lined paper before me.

> Alone, stung
> by death's visitation,
> teardrops indent the sheet
> that lies vacant.
> Grief gnaws as cruel as cold.
> Loss silences syllables, chokes
> meter, bitters hope.

Birdsong breaks sorrow's hold.

A crisp, curled, white oak leaf
drops to the dampened page.

> *I look up.*

A scarlet cardinal orchestrates
the rustle of dry brown leaves
like a Seneca Indian legend
defying winter's assault.

In the breeze I stand,
like an early jonquil bud
and like prayer, lift
a memory of you.

Why I Still Struggle with a Cloudless Sky
In Remembrance of 9/11

It's the irony that still twists my gut
when azure sky blankets
instead of gray clouds
in September, and I
remember Twin Towers.

Maybe my initial denial
haunts me, when the first
plane hit, on a TV screen
in a rheumatologist's
waiting room.

I peered between artificial plants
from a vinyl chair—
the aircraft seemed small
against the robin egg sky.

Maybe because *just an accident* fell
from my lips, *a tragedy,*
someone careless,
not terrorists, not here.

Maybe it was the eerie
coincidence of my calling
home, from the doctor's office
saying, I'm all right
at the same moment hundreds
were calling and saying, *I'm all right,*
when in an instant, they'd be gone

and I'm still here.

Maybe it was the shock
of seeing the second plane
packed with breath, broken
into Tower Two and my running
across the parking lot to my car
when the natural world gave no sigh
when I needed to be home to touch my kids
when I clung to the kinship on the radio, alone.

Maybe it was the opulent cerulean sky
without clouds or planes of its own
just televised pillars of dust and flames
a canvas for horror when nature
showed no sympathy
no rain.

And Yet the Weather Remains the Same
For Austin and Alexis

I implored the clouds to rain in torrents
but when the water didn't come
not even in a drizzle
I realized clouds had no
empathy to cry with me.

So, I urged the wind, begged
for a blast of arctic air
to make others shudder. Chill
all to the core so they would

possess that empty pit of frost
Grief forced me to swallow.
When none stirred, I beseeched
the sun believing that one scorch

would bend all to their knees
twisted in hot agony
and I would not kneel alone.
But the sun did not change

and you both are still gone.

At the Sequatchie Valley Scenic Overlook on Hwy 1 11 South

             I stop to breathe in the beauty
of dotted evergreens among the stripped
deciduous trees. Let my eyes sweep like a hang glider
off Lewis Chapel Mountain and soar over the valley floor,
             feeling the pull of flight, wingless.

I'm drawn up as the sunset peacocks.
Oranges, pinks, and yellows fan
like iridescence halos behind a pair of clouds.
.
             I steal comfort in fading light and autumn scent.
Linger for night's first star and wish this dusk with you.
Illusion extends your arm behind my back, pulls
my shoulders up to inhale the breeze that ruffles my hair
             your musk rising from dead leaves.

The Fish

I felt him tug—gripped the rod—stared
as the bobber dipped and line bent
while charged voices urged me to pull.

His form raised like a ghost
beneath the watery membrane—
his body over-whelmed by mine.

The fish burst through the veil—dangled
on clear thread—its scales sparked sun beams—
its gills struggled with empty air.

I'm stunned—too deaf to digest praise
for my first prize—*a small sunfish.*
Instead, I'm entranced by circles

in the water the fish and I
started—all that he knew behind—
all my learning in front of me.

My uncle nudged—placed the fish's
rough flesh—flat body—bulging eyes
and his last breath into my hands.

I flinched—dropped him to the bottom
of the boat—my cousin Stephen
nose-dived like a pelican—cupped

him and ripped free the thorny bait—
threw him with a host of others
in a pail—I stared at the lake.

They fried the fish with those they caught
and cleaned—to them I was silly
for not wanting to eat my catch.

I kneeled close to the dark water
in the campfire's shadows—plopped
pebbled sorrow in empty rings.

To Kyle at Fifteen

And I am here
with all your family
and friends on the grass.

The sun shines, the wind whips
the tent awning flaps' metal snaps
to clang against the poles like
swing chains at the playground.

You, once a boy
on a motorcycle.

Acquiescence

Silence in the face of atrocity is not neutrality;
silence in the face of atrocity is acquiescence.
Samantha Power

Canada geese force air to part,
migrate their bodies across gray skies,
rail their arrival with incessant cries.

I hear their intermittent honks from the lake.
They sing, despite the drone of rain slapping
against the window, gutters spilling over
like refugees at our southern borders.
No more room for the overflow.

Below on the eroding bank
geese waddle up the hill
toward my home
looking for food.

I offer nothing
but they stay

out of despair
          or hope

I can't say.

Never Say Never

Momma always emphasized, *Never say never*
or you'll do whatever you said you'd never

do, but at eighteen I knew I was clever
knew that marriage forever

with a man ten years older was wise—couldn't fail.
Knew I'd have a new home that would entail

beautiful kids, good job, happy life
all I fantasied with no strife

and I'd never divorce. Never replace
a wedded choice I embraced

but on year thirteen divorce I did. I ate my crow
because remember I said I would never you know

and I swore I'd never eat it again.
No, I'd never marry again, but then

at forty I forgot and married a man fifteen years younger
vowing that this time I'd never put asunder

a man who appreciated stability
and would be potent in his virility

but women proved not to be his stimulation
and eating crow became my preoccupation

so I chewed louder—enjoyed irony's bitter cast
until he came, a high school sweetheart from my past

and though I'd proclaimed, *I'll never again marry*
now fifty and convinced this love would never vary

so sure Momma's words did not apply
and after all what was one more try?

I'll never divorce again,
                              but I did.

Mariposa de la Muerte
For Eloisa

You're harmless like a loose strand of hair,
a creature reborn donning black
velvet wings, thin like parchment,
where intricate patterns lace,
zig-zag back and forth,
pulled into darkness

and to ripened fruit
or drawn to the light
against the ceiling fixture
frantic, flapping like darting eyes.
Your shadow looms in the house
like the rattle fluttering in her chest.

My Ex Hides in the Corners of My Poems Like a Cat

          arches his back,
stretches his body
against my memory,
purrs around my legs,
until, I almost trip.

I attempt to put him out of mind.

Draw the blinds, hide
the windows of my soul,

but at night his shadow slips
between the slats of a sonnet
like the light from the lamppost
                         on the street.

My inner landlord says stop feeding him.
He will go away—
as if starving a cat is easy.

I try to write prose,
something deep and serious
to chase him away,
but when I opened a can
of poetry, he paws
my door and slinks
in, licking his fur in satisfaction
boldly shedding on my plush verse.

Today I find him
rolled and content, sleeping
in my finest haiku,

and I want to put him out again…

but it is cold
and I'm lonely
and he loves me—
at least that's
what I tell myself.

**Driving Up Lewis Chapel Mountain from Dunlap,
Tennessee, before Nightfall**

Like colored yarn cut in a rug,
magenta threads streak
and twist through hues
of deep violet, orange, and gold,
basting stars against a growing seam
of gray backing above the plateau.

Halfway up the mountain, I could have pulled
over to the overlook, counted the strokes
night needed to sweep dusk under its feet,
but no. I headed home.
There will be other sunsets I assured
myself, knowing we are never promised one.

A Classic

The scene plays in my head
like a movie in black and white.
You, behind the Queen Anne,
your hands knead the upholstery.

 I, the wife, suspect nothing.

You utter lines to move the scene.
We need to talk, and *I know it's not a good time.*
A worn matinee plot often seen
on an old theater projector.

The camera tightens on you.
Then the dramatic pause
right before the climax:

                    I'm leaving.

On cue, I drop
to the floor and sob,
as the volume rises
to cacophony.

The first celluloid
section stops,
but the reel keeps
spinning,

and the sound
of the free end
slaps over
and over.

Ghosts

Perhaps a refracted light ignites
a play of shadow in the doorway,
compels your synapses to fill in
an image in the brain when
no one is there in the home.

It's just an ocular disturbance
you tell yourself to say,
but the reverberating chill groans
throughout your body despite
an educated mind of disbelief.

Sometimes a wisp of cologne
like musk flicks a projection before you
makes memory manufacture
a zone of fancy to thrill the eye
like the quick flare of a match in the dark.

And even though careful not to fan
the flame or fuel the apparition
with your startled apprehension
you continue to stare at nothing there
unable to fight the tick of your own heart.

And if for relief you're looking,
if the need to explain, blame
something you ate or a tale you read
too late at night, you will continue to bemoan,
even *though this defies all I've known, I feel I'm not alone.*

Our Fab Four
After The Beatles

I used to be eleven yesterday,
fifty-three years ago and I would sing
through the album,
Sgt Pepper's Lonely Hearts Club Band
with my sister Roxane,
my cousin Judson, both nine,
and my cousin Vicki, who was probably four.

Our stage, an open sleeping bag,
flannel side-up. Our go-go boots,
white tube socks. Our microphone,
a pink hairbrush tossed back and forth
as we each sometimes sang,
more often lip synced
solos and duets waxing
the whole album trying to groove
with the beat or weave our bodies
to the psychedelic strains
of the sitar and sarangi never anticipating
the group would split and marry
or that John would be shot by a delusional man.

When our families came together to watch
our show, we sang without wondering
what Ringo meant about getting high,
never questioned *Lucy in the Sky with Diamonds'* lyrics
but we welcomed *the one and only Billy Shears* with wide
arms, swaying in fringed vests and bell-bottom jeans
mouthing *When I'm 64* as if it would never happen.

Trying to Explain What It Is Like to Survive a Broken Heart
After "Purple Rain" by Prince

…it's like steering your car on a narrow switchback
two lane road on an unfamiliar mountain through a storm

and there's a rain with wind—a gale that topples trees
floods tributaries of the soul…

it's a torrential downpour that spiders and splats, scurries
into new positions on the windshield,
distorts what lies ahead…

then conditions worsen—black ice through banks of fog
you creep, crawl, claw, forward on the never ending asphalt
and the instant you praise yourself for moving
.
his voice becomes the radio…
I never meant to cause you any sorrow…

your flashers on, your eyes aimed low
straining to keep on the right side of the white line
yellow lines blur, caught in advancing highway halos—

his voice croons, *I never meant to cause you any pain.*

You clutch the wheel staring through the windshield
wind whipped—pelted with hail
that wipers can't appease.
.
And all you can do—
                     must do—
                              is drive.

What We Accept

                          Mushrooms ribbon in scalloped ridges
                    along a ragged fissure where the wood splits
              where the water seams
the creosote soaked spine of Douglas fir.
And the toxins dream in rivulets—
       spread like tendrils.
            of oily sheen
                in tar-filtered channels.
               And the ghost tree,
           once railroad timber,
      just acquiesces
leaning on river rocks.
And the lichens, like the mushrooms
       teem on the lumber's saturated core,
           tasting not, what leaches from the layers,
              tingling not, when the poison penetrates.

Time Measurement

Out,
as fog
unfurling
like candle string,
thin like tatted lace,
clouding blue morning sky,
teasing the way lilac scent
pillows April's early breezes,
spring makes death seem a distant fair,
a fluttery thought, quick to dissipate,
like the blossom of orange lilies
or mayflies who live a day
or man who struts briefly.
Chronos spins.
A wick's cut.
Flame goes
out.

Reflection
For WGW

Winter etches frost
in cryptic crystal patterns
glazes over panes.

Light skates across glass,
preens cold arcs like sparks
that signal in the sun.

Dazzled by sparkle
forgetting, for a second
thoughts of death and loss.

Haphazard melting
smears like welts on scarred skin,
Ice drops. Mimics tears.

A gust of wind chill
catches breath's moment
and fades in gray dusk.

Bar Room Meditating

In the style of John C. Mannone

Like serrated flames//amber licks crystal cut glass in bar light/
the lowball burns against my spurned flesh cold//numbing// I
play coy//swirl the mix of Knob Creek and refracting ice// not
neat//appreciate the high-pitch clink of change in glass// pass
the aged spirits by my nostrils//delay the weighted words on
my tongue//stroke the scent of nuts and oak and vanilla spice
//slide the slow sip between parted lips//ruminate on the bold
Burn down the back of my throat//good whiskey is never bitter
//like divorce

What Mama Bears
For Margo

And for a moment,
I cuddle your memory.
Imagine you just a babe,
my hands, baby lotion coated,
and you, a squirming delight, wiggling
across the towel, giggling at the game.

Tonight, I bundle myself in a large blanket
adorned with a silhouette of a mama bear against
a background of cream. The hem checkered like
reality in black and white.

The bear, bold
across my chest, as if to protect me.
I let her do what I could not do,
                       for you

This bear can't thwart the cold
any more than it could have torn the noose
you used to quell the darkness from
                       your neck.

Under this comforter, I twist, *if only's*—drag
unearned serrated guilt across this hollow
ache, maul retrospect—as if it, and I, by force,
could bring you back whole, instead of in ash.

I cuddle your memory,
even though it bites back.

Unrequited

And then to want and not have—to want and want—how that
wrung the heart, and wrung it again and again.
        Virginia Woolf, *To the Lighthouse*

If I weave my yearning for you into a basket,
thin willow strips bend in place so tight
that my hunger squeezes like a python
wound and bound as constrictive as a tourniquet.

Thin willow strips bend in place so tight
that air struggles to pass through the crevices.
Wound and bound as constrictive as a tourniquet,
the ache twists in and out, over and under.

Air struggles to pass through the crevices.
Collected tears won't leak out.
The ache twists in and out, over and under
and the want never comes to an end.

Even collected tears won't leak out
when my hunger squeezes like a python.
If I weave my yearning for you into a basket,
the want will never come to an end.

Wind

How you tease. Caress
my skin like a scarf, silken and light.

The scent of new green
the flutter like breath

against the nape of my neck.
Windchimes stir. Woo the silent

air with a familiar voice.
No clouds in the dusted blue,

just you.

And I forget the red-streaked
morning, the earlier storms,

floods, damage,
and trust

you once more
in the night.

When July Lingers

Fading light casts a honey glaze
to shadowed alcoves. Your waiting

silhouette, an illusion, on the veranda.
Echoes of castanets prompt remembrance

as I recall the click of my heels,
the rush up the stairs to you.

Even tonight as my blue veined
right hand clutches the wrought iron rail

my left hand, gathers the ghost
of a full skirt. I lean on the stucco arch

at the landing. Summer heat ignites
carnation's scent in balcony boxes.

I recall my body's rise in your embrace,
The tango of our lust. Your words promising

forever, never conceiving that memory's
eternity was all I'd possess.

When the Universe Offers a Sign

Everything changes, even stone.
Claude Monet

I found a river rock shaped like a tornado,
large enough to fill my palm,
broad at the top, narrow at the bottom,
gray like storm clouds twisted with striations.

It feels solid and strong—
everything I didn't feel
after you left.

I hold it tight like the grip
of a pistol, the thickest part
butted between my thumb
and forefinger.

I hope for strength.
I squeeze the stone
and all fingers point to me.

I put that rock aside
and look for another—
something more like
the color of your eyes.

Oh, Autumn

Death grays the ground in increments
steals time and light, expects
each of us to cower in his coming—
but not you.

You rail maples red
and blast smoke trees orange.
You melt yellow poplar like ripened pears,
from green to gold to dark honey.

Pumpkins rise among dying vines.
Granny apples, Macintoshes, Ambrosias
fuel the air mulled with cinnamon,
cloves and sugar.

You host the gallivant of goblins,
rustle music out of fallen leaves.
Offer a banquet of chrysanthemums—
maroon, purple and lemon blossomed.

Oh Autumn,
You who will not shroud in death
until winter takes its mantel, fight.

In the Dead of Winter by the Lake

Heat steals from day's cache
leaves chill to play in shadows
off lake's broken shore.

Submerged weeds rise
in ragged rows below
the shape of a malformed tree,

a folded creature
made to draw in water
like a mastodon's trunk

from a primordial age.
Its branches thin, splayed,
a madman's array

of naked limbs, void of leaves
and buds, void of birds
or bugs—dormant or dead.

Below knotted roots,
planted gray rocks serve
in place of vegetation.

Beyond, water sounds
in quiet mumbles
above silence's whisper.

The sun bleached of color
burns lines across the water
like ruled paper,

and I ache for spring.

Spellbound

Future leans in the doorway // shrouds herself // in smokey-spirals like those drifting from unfiltered cigarettes // found in ill-lit rooms where music plays and she sways to undulating rhythms // sometimes blues // sometimes jazz // Her silhouette full and curvaceous // seamed in a low-cut // black// empire-waisted dress // titillating me with the perfume of possibilities // And I know she's a tease // leaves me waiting outside the door as she sashays back and forth//bending toward me // with a hint from her ample bodice making me lean // eyes straining to glimpse her ripe offerings // And I want to believe in her // for us //that this time she won't be fickle // that she will provide all she seems // solely to me // and not to every other dreamer in the room // so I sit and wait for some glimpse // beyond her thin // semi-translucent veils // tantalized by all manner of her exotic intimations // I am stymied by the desire to know her // limited by inaction // in hope that she'll unfold // expose herself to me // in some moment of vulnerability // and give me the impetus to move.

Salvation

Heavy with dark ruminations
I walk to escape myself
along a waist-high stone wall
overgrown with English Ivy.

Rose of Sharon and Crepe Myrtle
burdened with blossom bow.
Their weighted limbs obscure
the outline of a path.

I plow head downward, litter
the clustered flowers, leave a wake
of petals indifferent to the beauty
of small things, not expecting her tucked

under the branches. The folds of her cement
gown traced in lichen. Her hands poised
in prayer, her face molded in sweetness
as if pleased that I should I find her there.

I host a smile. Reach to pull
the ivy from her solid feet, release
thorny brambles that crown
around her dress
as if I was there for her
when she had been waiting
                              for me.

Special Thanks

Had I not reached out to my Thursday Night Ekphrastic Group in 2020, it's unlikely that many of the poems within this book would have been written. To Becky Briar, Heather Davis, Pat Hope, Laura Miller, Sherry Poff, Wes Sims, Jennifer Smith, and Ray Zimmerman, with a hearty dose of praise for our leader, John C Mannone, I owe much thanks. Thanks also to the critical eyes of John C. Mannone, Sue Dunlap, and Susan Underwood who spirited this manuscript into a form. Thanks to my friend Sharon Shaddrick who patiently listened to my poems when I was editing. Thanks to Zach Burnette for his line editing. Beverly Key for her photography and Stephanie Tate for her cover. Thanks always to my children, Nathan and Tricia for their continued encouragement.

Natalie Kimbell was born in Norton, Virginia, spent her early elementary school years in Worcester, Massachusetts, and then moved to Dunlap, Tennessee to find her home. She is a 1978 graduate of Sequatchie County High School and a 1982 graduate of the University of Tennessee at Chattanooga. She serves as an English and theater arts and creative writing instructor at her high school alma mater. This year, 2025, marks her forty-first and last full-time year as an educator.

Although writing most of her life, she only began releasing her writing in 2017. Since then, her work has placed in several contests, anthologies and has appeared in publications such as the *Appalachian Writers Anthology, Women Speak, Pine Mountain Sand and Gravel, Artemis, Shift* as well as in *The Mildred Haun Review* and *Tennessee Voices Anthology.* Though primarily a poet, Kimbell has also published creative nonfiction and ten-minute monologues.